# THE FANTASTIC FRIDGE FRENZY

## A GREENIE FAMILY ADVENTURE

By Corri Cooper Scott

Illustrated by Amanda Letcher

Dedicated to my two peanuts who ignited my love
of children's books and my quest for healthy eating.

Not long after Chef Charlie's trip to the grocery store, an adventure began in the refrigerator of her kitchen.

Inside the refrigerator lived a special family.
The Greenies were a produce family consisting of
Broccoli Bob, Carrot Carol, Apple Allie, and Avocado Andy.

The Greenies lived a happy, chilled life on the top shelf inside the refrigerator.

That all changed the day Chef Charlie returned from the grocery store with a bag of fresh groceries.

As Chef Charlie unpacked the green beans, yogurt, bananas, and other healthy foods from her shopping bag, the Greenies froze with fear!

Apple Allie was afraid she'd be replaced with a fresh apple and separated from her family. "Will I be moved into the crisper drawer?" she asked worriedly.

And Avocado Andy was scared he would be moved to the compost bin to live with worms!

Broccoli Bob scratched his leafy head with concern, needing to come up with a plan to keep his family together. He knew he had to act quickly before Chef Charlie replaced them with new produce!

He had an idea!

String cheese!

Broccoli Bob tore open the plastic-wrapped string cheese and began shredding it into thin rope-like pieces. He tied the pieces together with knots and planned his family's escape route.

Using their newly constructed string cheese rope, the Greenies shimmied down from the top shelf of the refrigerator.

Soon, Broccoli Bob, Carrot Carol, Apple Allie, and Avocado Andy all landed safely on the lower shelf.

"We made it!" they cheered.

Carrot Carol told her family to quickly hide behind the milk carton as she heard Chef Charlie begin to open the refrigerator door.

Chef Charlie began moving the new groceries into the refrigerator, looking for wilted veggies to remove.

The Greenies were nervous as they hid quietly.

After Chef Charlie placed the last item from the bag into the refrigerator, she finally closed the door.

The Greenies were safe! They knew they would stay together and chill happily ever after.

Until . . .

Mold set in!